Jobs People Do

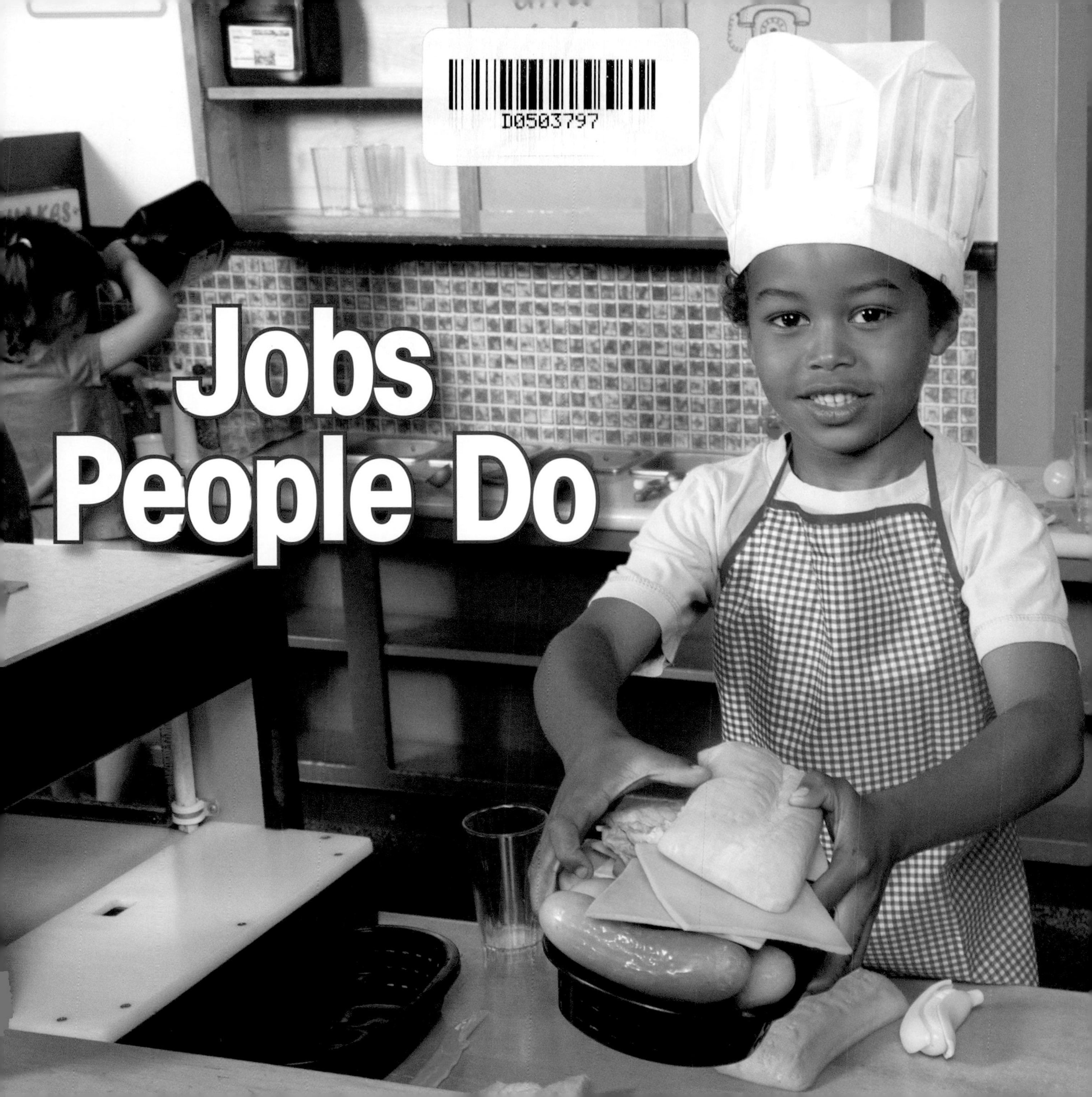

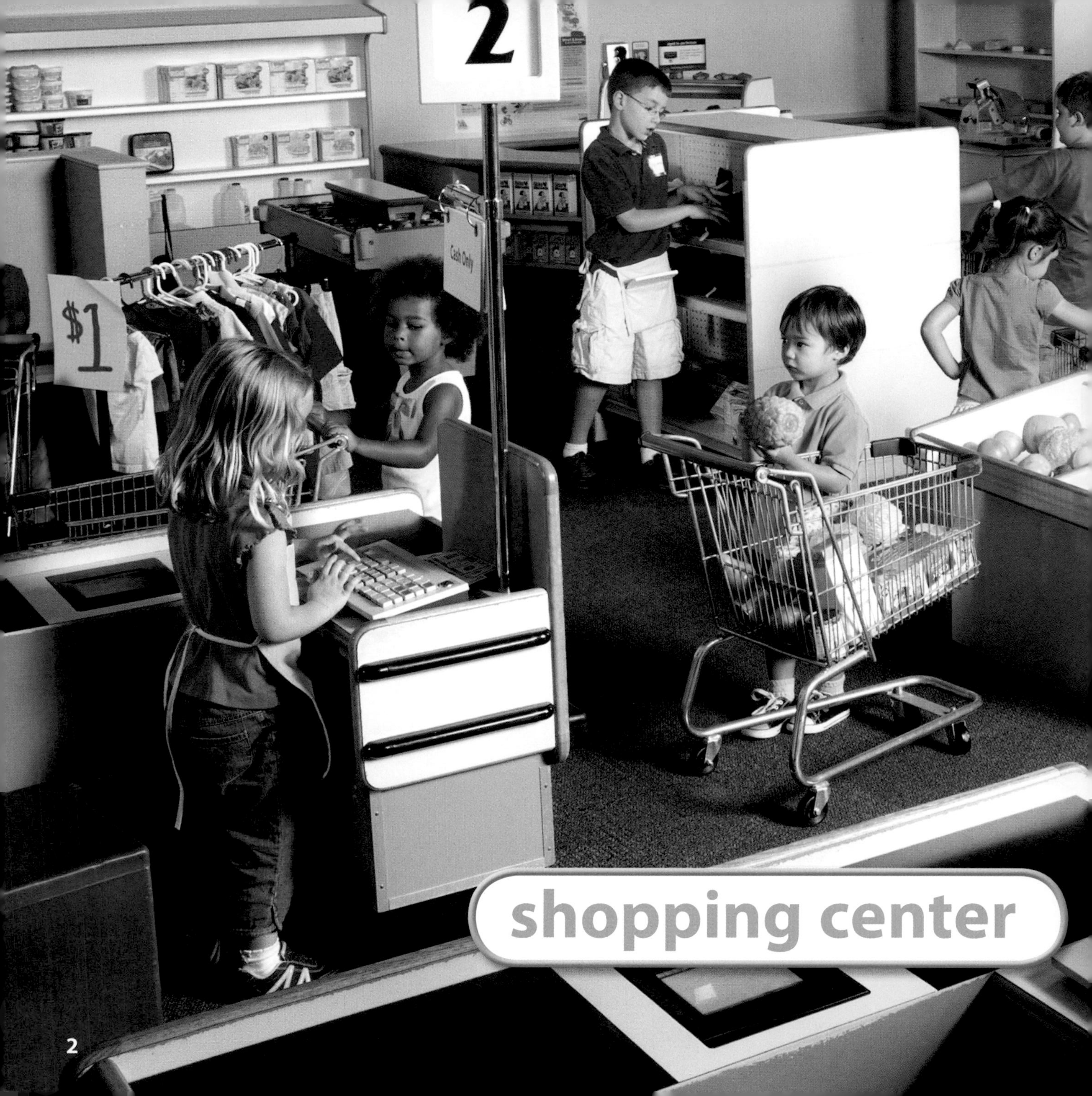

shopping center

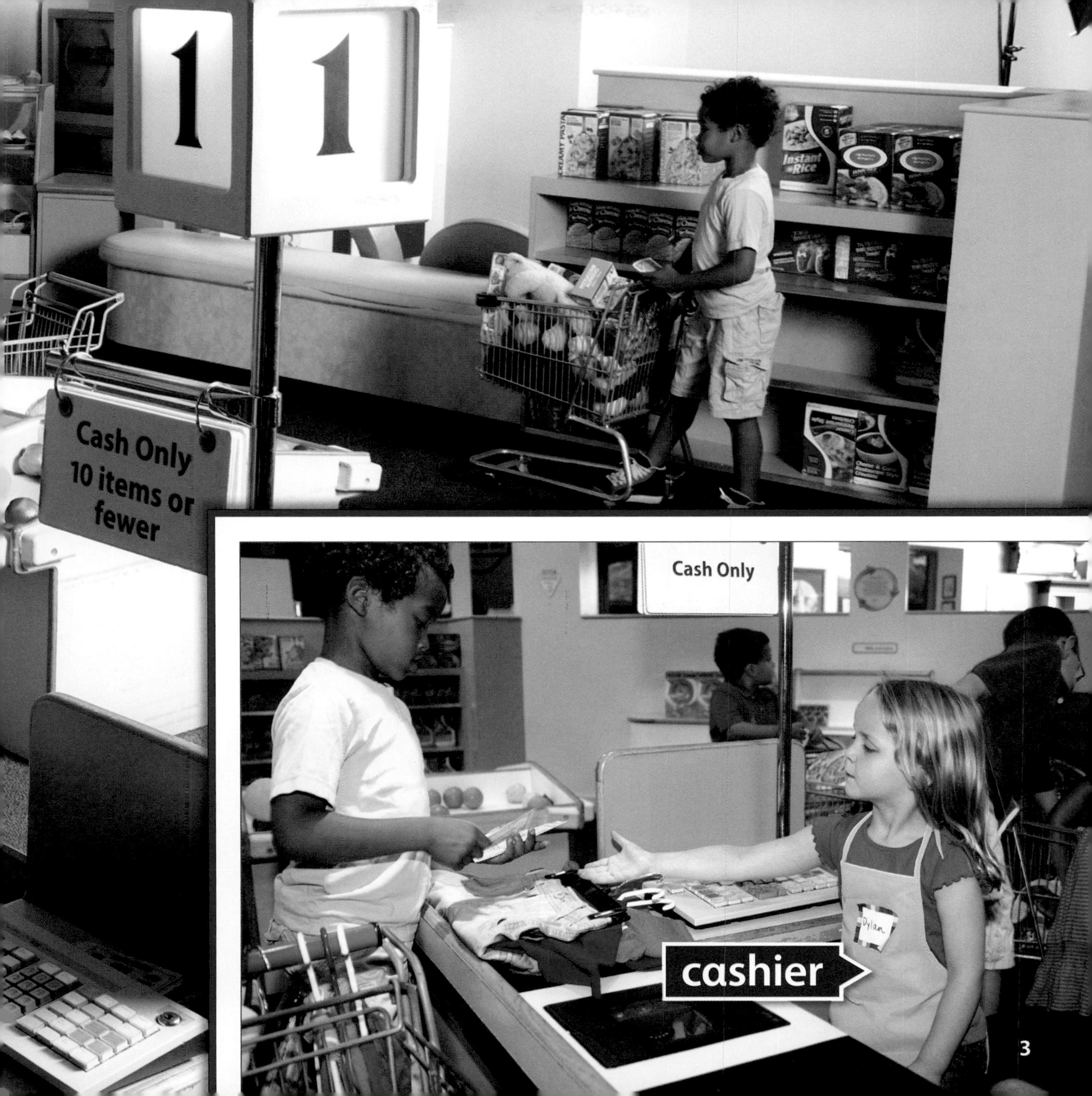
1
1
Cash Only
10 items or fewer
Creamy Pasta
Instant Rice
Cash Only
cashier
Dylan

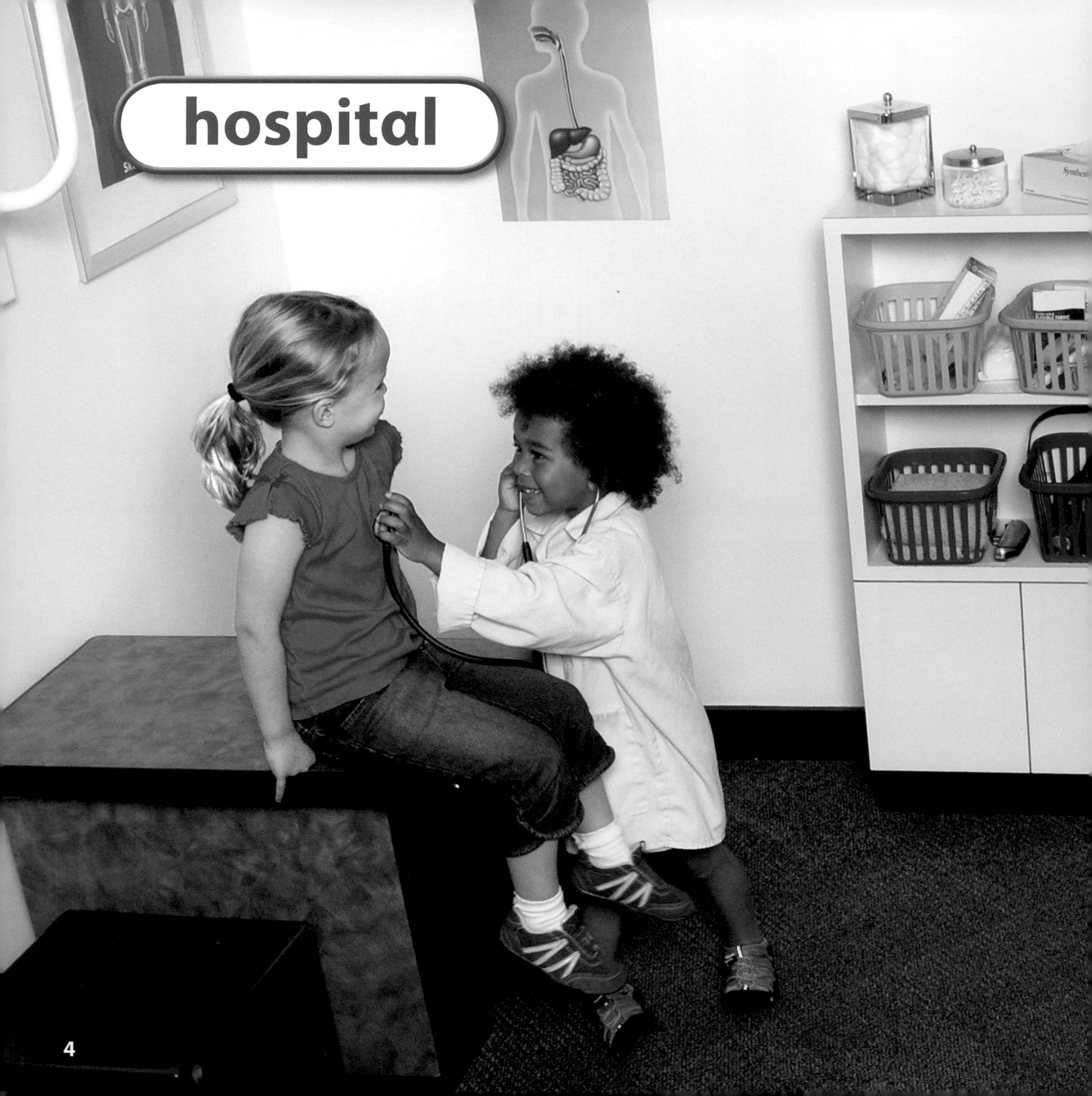

hospital

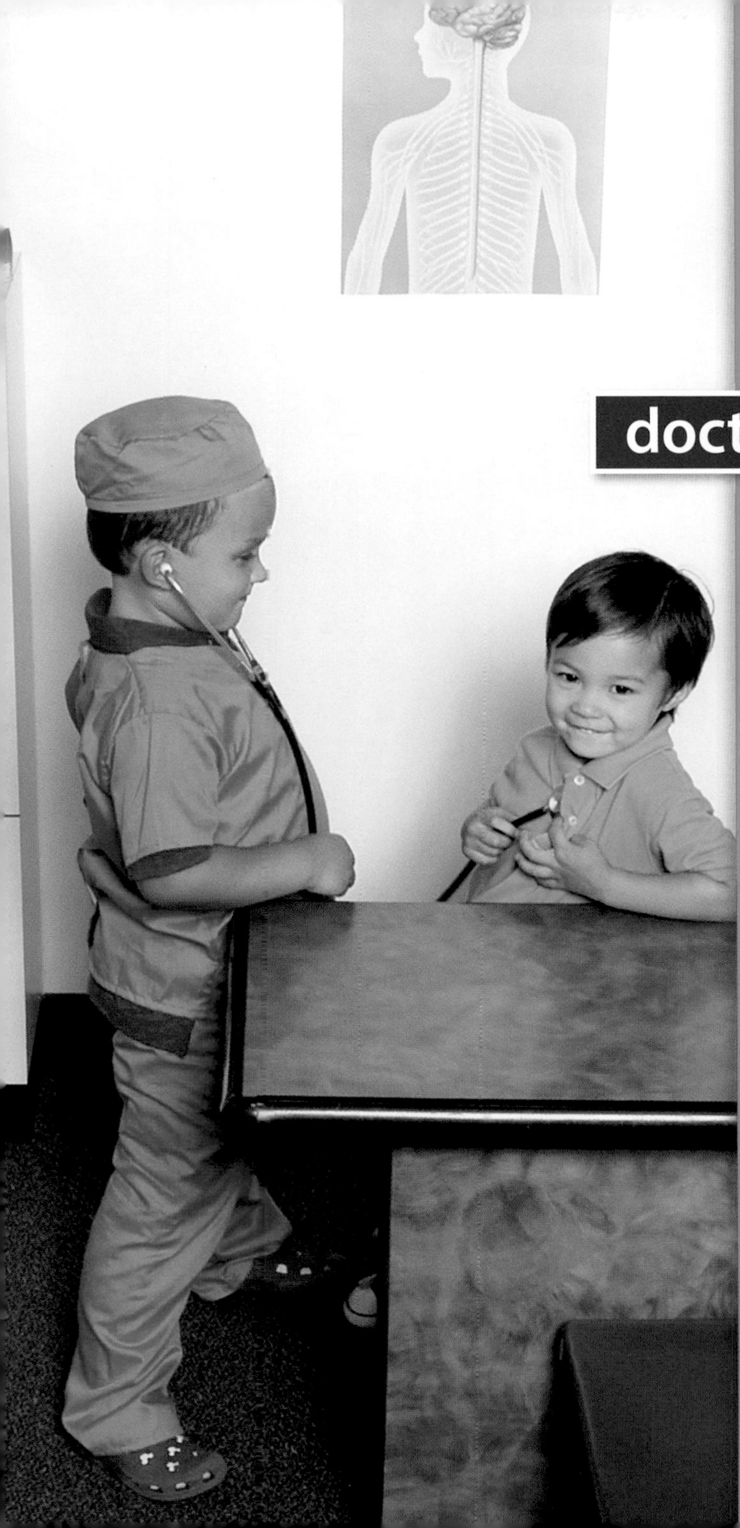

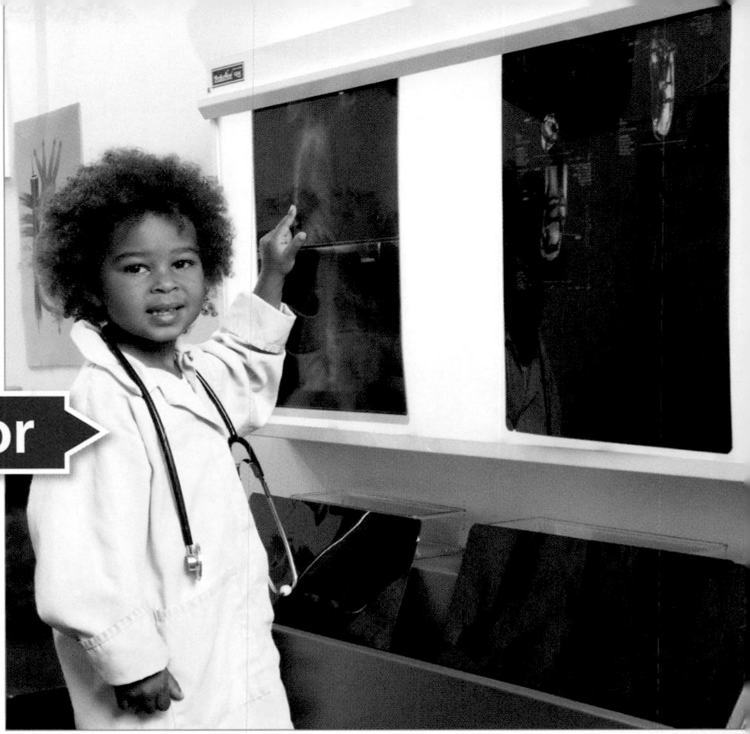
doctor

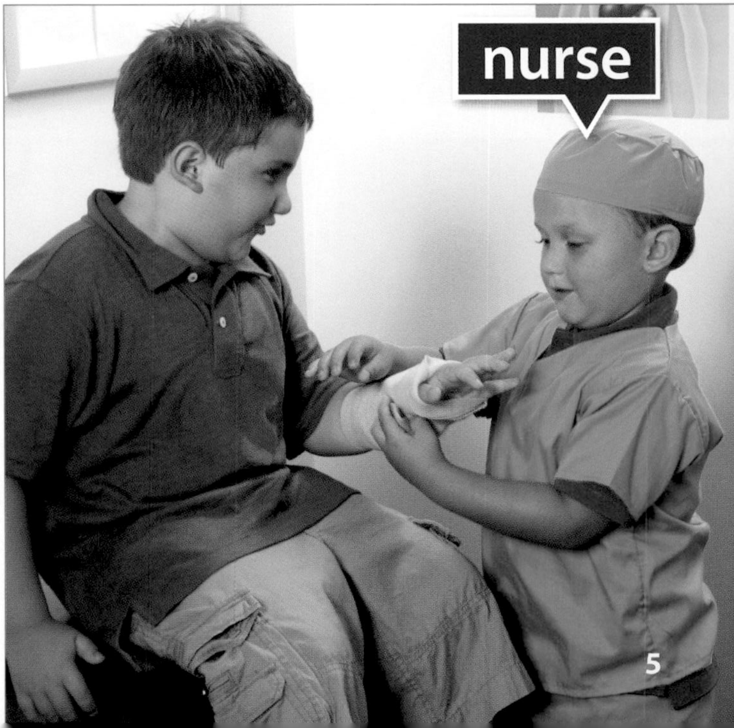
nurse

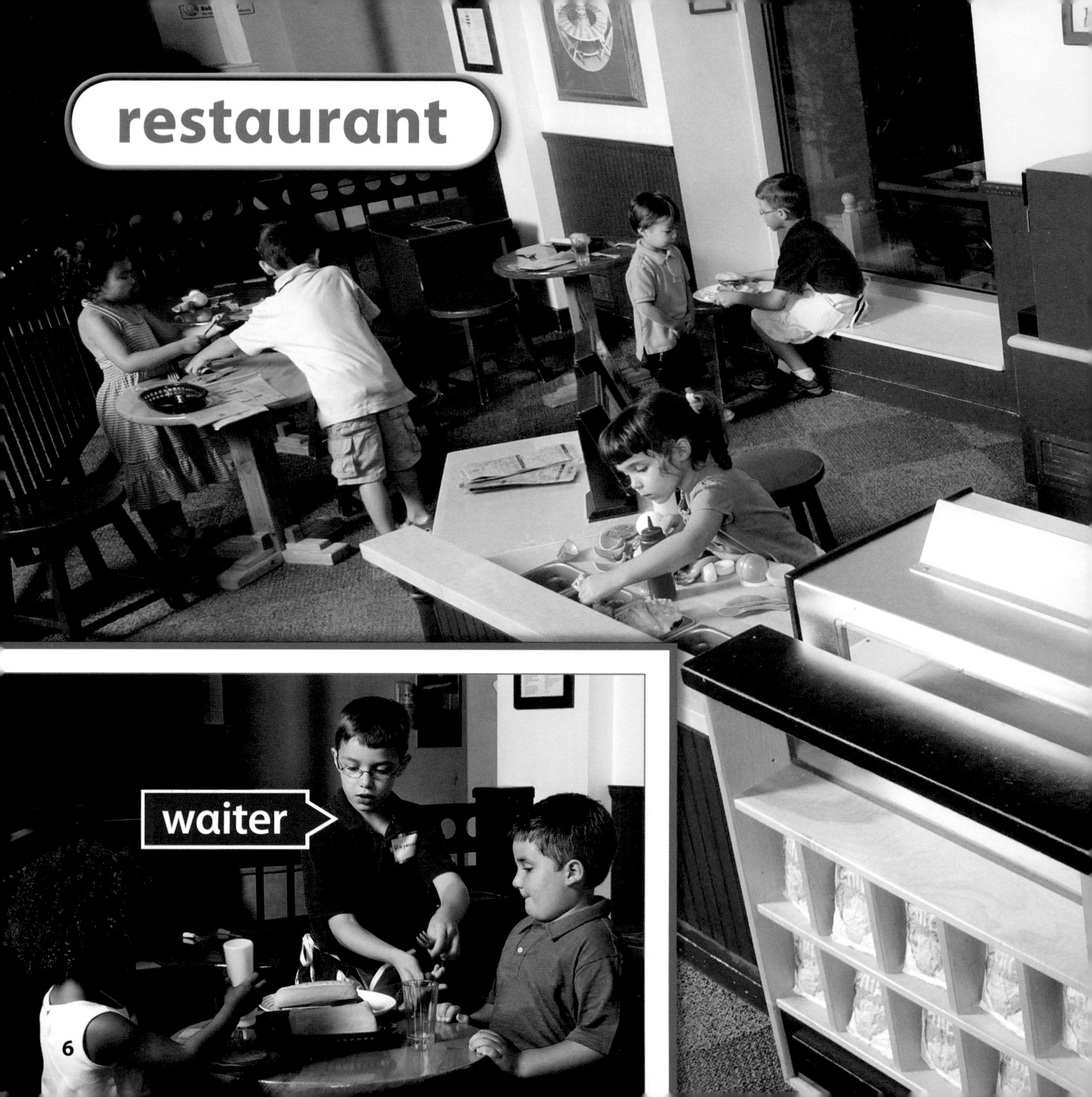
restaurant
waiter

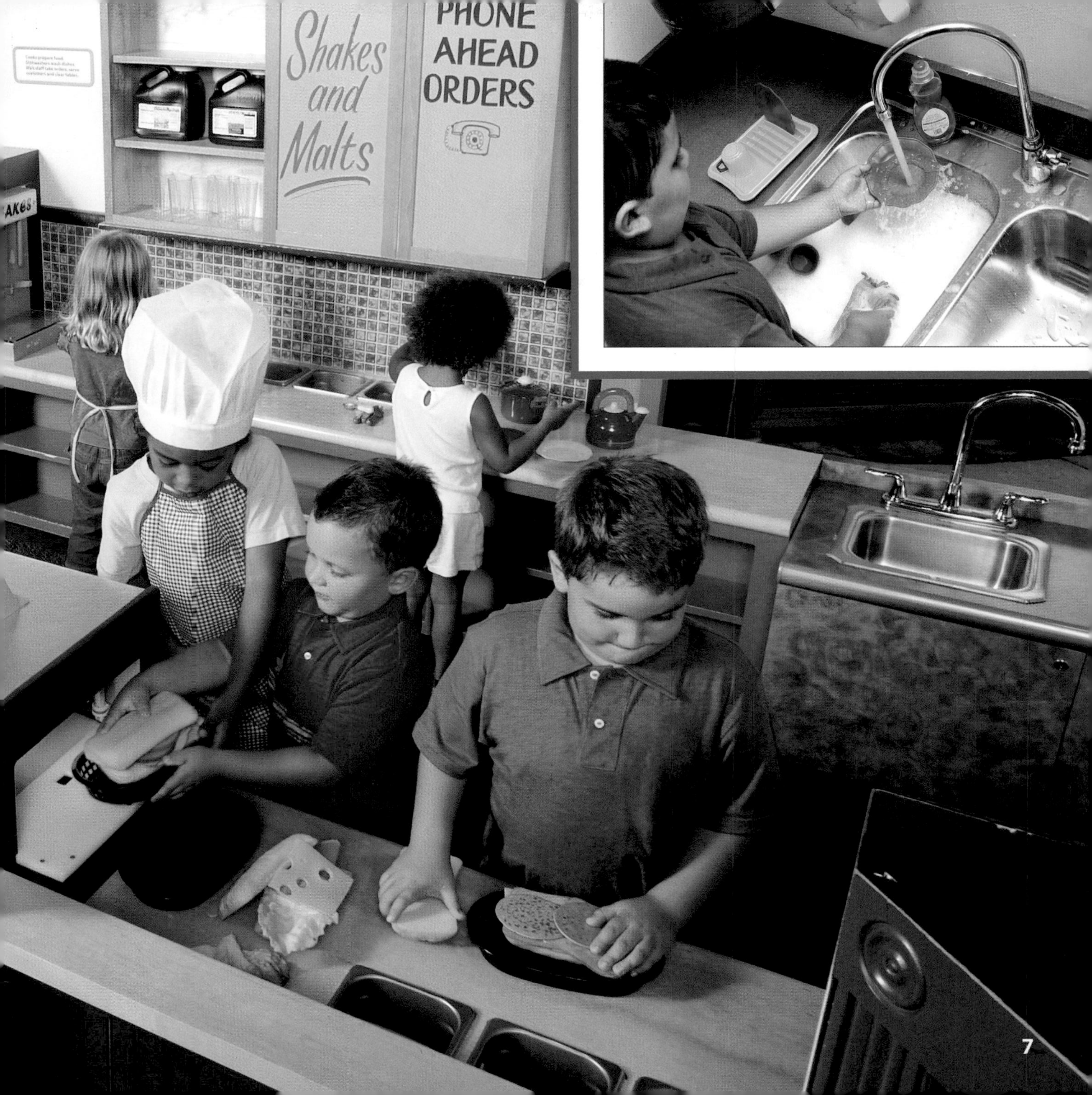
Shakes
and
Malts
PHONE
AHEAD
ORDERS

I want to be a . . .

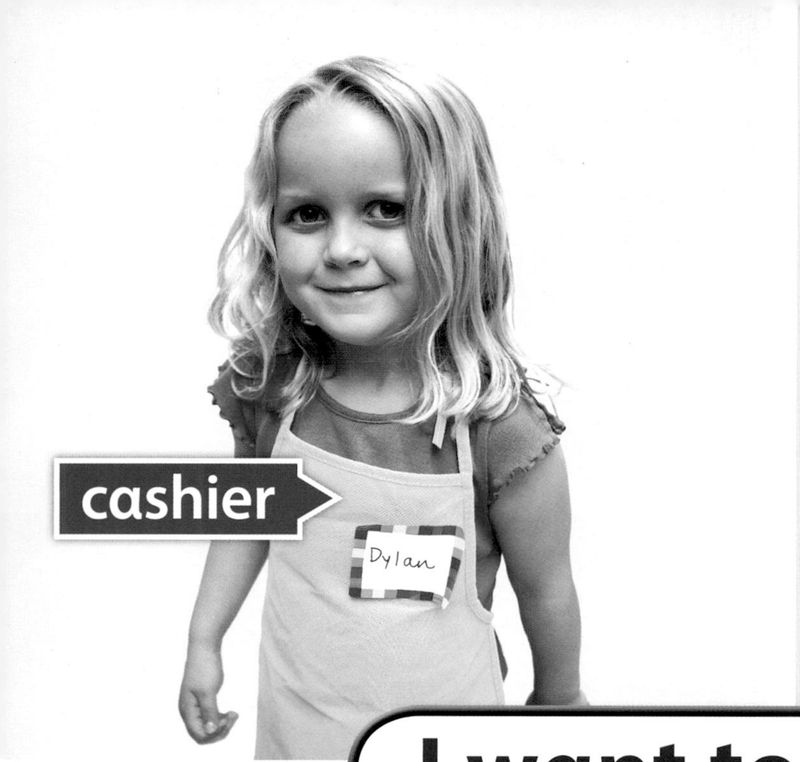

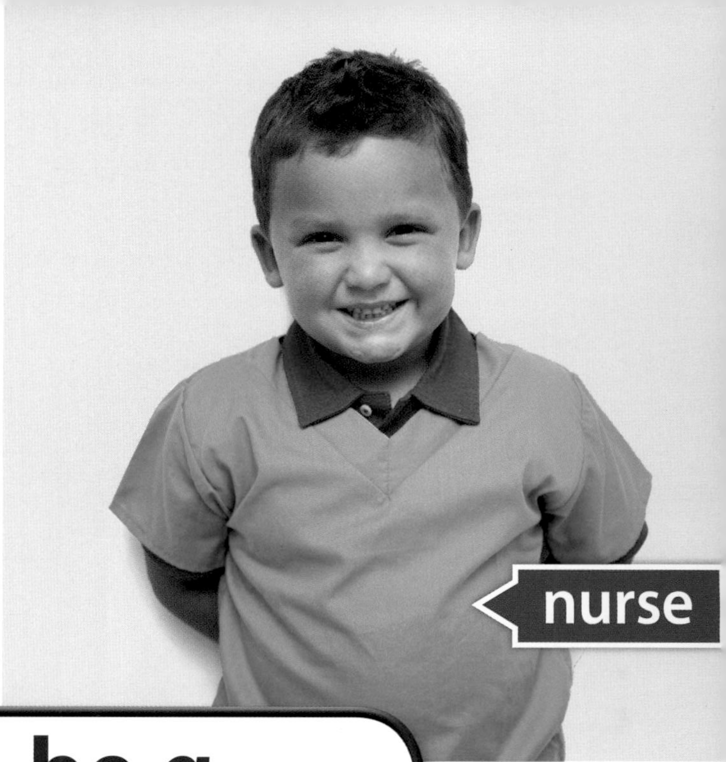

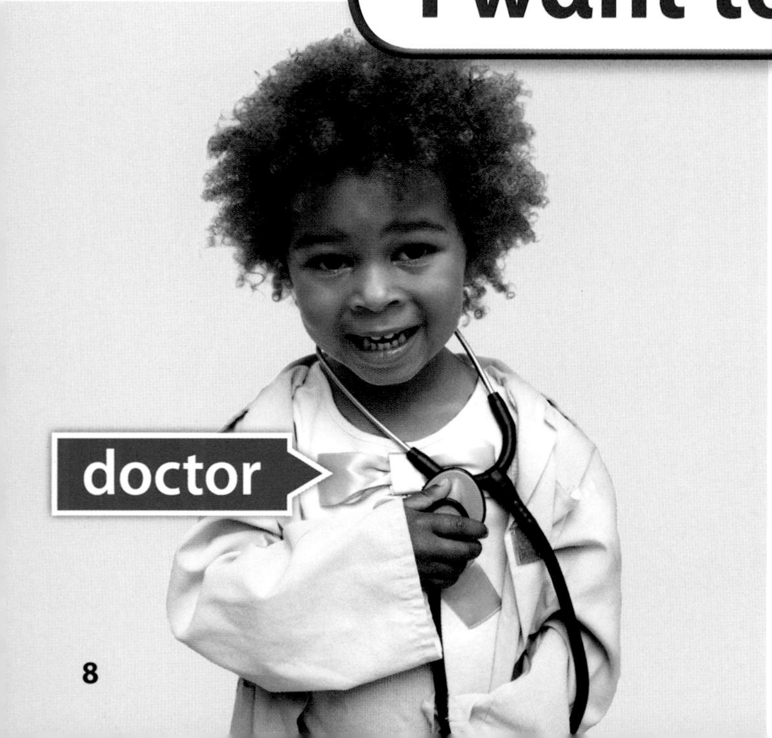

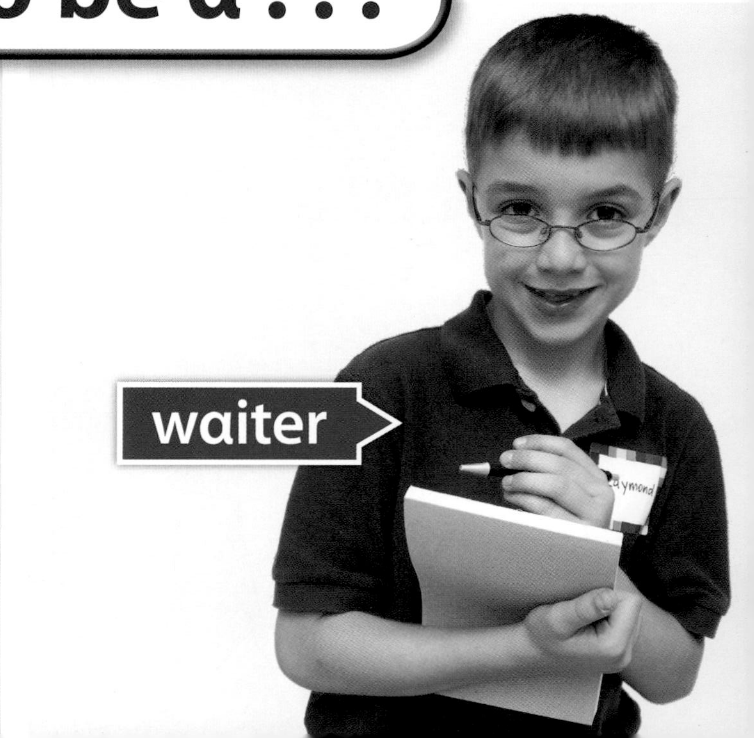